I WILL ARISE

Biblical Characters who Arose from
Failure to Spiritual Victory

by
Lloyd D. Grimm, Jr.

AUTHOR OF

Called to be a Pastor

Great is Thy Faithfulness

Sixty-Six Days, Sixty-Six Books

"I Will Arise..."

(St. Luke 15:18)

SCHMUL PUBLISHING COMPANY
NICHOLASVILLE, KENTUCKY

Published by Schmul Publishing Co.
PO Box 776
Nicholasville, KY USA

Printed in the United States of America

ISBN 10: 0-88019-590-8
ISBN 13: 978-0-88019-590-4

Visit us on the Internet at www.wesleyanbooks.com, or order direct from the publisher by calling 800-772-6657, or by writing to the above address.

Contents

Foreword

As Christians we are engaged in a very real spiritual warfare. God's Word admonishes us to "Put on the whole armor of God, that ye may be able to stand against the wiles of the devil. For we wrestle not against flesh and blood, but against principalities, against powers, against the rulers of the darkness of this world, against spiritual wickedness in high places." (Ephesians 6:11-12.) The apostle Paul in writing to Timothy expresses this concept of spiritual warfare as he exhorts this young pastor to "...endure hardness, as a good soldier of Jesus Christ" (II Timothy 2:3).

According to the inspired Word of God the norm for the spirit filled children of God is that they should live a wholly sanctified life for we read, "But as he which hath called you is holy, so be ye holy in all manner of conversation; Because it is written, Be ye holy; for I am holy" (I Peter 1:15-16).

Although provision is made for us to live a victorious holy life (Hebrews 13:12) yet many fall short. The casualty rate is far too high in our battle against the forces of evil. This treatise is not to promote, accept or expect defeat while

4

fighting the "good fight of faith" but to encourage any who have fallen in battle to take courage remembering the scripture in I John 2:1-2, "My little children these things write I unto you, that ye sin not. And if any man sin, we have an advocate with the Father, Jesus Christ the righteous: And He is the propitiation for our sins: And not for ours only, but also for the sins of the whole world."

So as heart breaking as it is to see one fall from the arms of our blessed Lord and Saviour Jesus Christ; there is recovery if we take up the cross and do the first works over. "If we confess our sins, He is faithful and just to forgive us our sins, and to cleanse us from all unrighteousness" (I John 1:9).

If one loses a battle he need not lose the war. The following in this booklet are Biblical characters who lost battles but made a "comeback" and were victorious in their spiritual conquest. None should despair who are truly seeking after God. "For I know the thoughts that I think toward you, saith the Lord, thoughts of peace, and not of evil, to give you an unexpected end. Then shall ye call upon me, and ye shall go and pray unto me, and I will hearken unto you. And ye shall seek me, and find me, when ye shall search for me with all your heart. And I will be found of you, saith the Lord" (Jeremiah 29:11-14).

—Lloyd D. Grimm, Jr.

1
SIMON PETER: Overconfidence

"Now Peter sat without in the palace: and a damsel came unto him, saying, Thou also wast with Jesus of Galilee. But he denied before them all, saying, I know not what thou sayest. And when he was gone out into the porch, another maid saw him, and said unto them that were there. This fellow was also with Jesus of Nazareth. And again he denied with an oath, I do not know the man. And after awhile came unto him they that stood by, and said to Peter, Surely thou also art one of them; for thy speech bewrayeth thee. Then began he to curse and swear, saying, I know not the man. And immediately the cock crew. And Peter remembered the word of Jesus, which said unto him, Before the cock crow Thou shalt deny me thrice. And he went out, and wept bitterly." —Matthew 26:69-75

OUR BELOVED GENERAL SUPERINTENDENT of the Church of the Nazarene, Dr. J.B. Chapman told of an experience he had when he was scheduled to follow a speaker who spoke on the subject, "Guarding Your Weaknesses." Dr. Chapman said he followed the first speaker by using for his subject, "Guarding Your Strengths."

While it is surely wise and in order to be diligent and on guard in areas where we are most vulnerable, God's army should always be on alert realizing we are opposed by a relentless subtle enemy that can and will change his tactics to further his cause. In Ephesians 6:11 this is spoken of as "the wiles of the devil." One of these wiles used by Satan in order to conquer those who follow Jesus is to catch one off guard resulting in an ambush. This is what happened in the case of Peter's denial. This apostle had become overconfident, and the enemy used a sneak attack in an attempt to completely destroy him.

The writer was a teenager at the time when World War II took place. I well remember sitting by a radio on a Sunday afternoon, Dec. 7, 1941, listening as the news filtered in that the Japanese were attacking Pearl Harbor. Congress was in session taking action to go to war with Japan. Those were dark days for our country, but why? Could this disaster have been avoided? If my memory serves me correctly, Japan had a delegation right here in the USA supposedly to work out problems and differences on a diplomatic level. No doubt that bred overconfidence. Also I understand a warning had taken place, but evidently it was either ignored or not taken seriously. Some of us still remember the aftermath of this tragedy, and the suffering our nation experienced.

We as Christians are engaged in a spiritual war (Ephesians 6:10-15), the outcome being more important than any war which has or will take place on this planet, for the results will not be for time but for eternity. St. Peter was a strong leader in the early Church. His name signifies a rock. When Jesus was catechizing His disciples as to their credentials asking them, "Whom say ye that I am? And Simon Peter answered and said, Thou art the Christ, the son of the living God" (Matthew 16:15-16). Then in verse

18 Jesus responded by saying, "And I say also unto thee, That thou art Peter, and upon this rock I will build my church; and the gates of hell shall not prevail against it." Christ's church is built on the confession of this truth, rather than on the Apostle Peter. But it was Peter who was living so close to God that the Holy Spirit was enabled to reveal the Divinity of Christ to him. Yet, Peter fell from this high spiritual standing when assailed by Satan.

Also, Peter was one of the inner circle of Disciples consisting of Peter, James, and John. It was this trio our Savior chose to accompany him on special occasions. They were present on the Mount of Transfiguration and called on to lend their support when our Redeemer suffered in the garden of Gethsemane. We read the account in St. Matthew 26:37-38. "And He took with Him Peter and the two sons of Zebedee, and began to be sorrowful and very heavy. Then saith He to them, My soul is exceeding sorrowful, even unto death: tarry ye here and watch with me."

Peter was a strong spiritual leader serving as a leader of leaders. Still it was this great man who failed by way of overconfidence. Before it took place Jesus told His Disciples that "All ye shall be offended because of me this night: for it is written, I will smite the shepherd, and the sheep of the flock shall be scattered abroad… Peter answered and said unto Him, though all men shall be offended because of Thee, yet will I never be offended…" Our Savior then said, "Verily I say unto thee, That this night, before the cock crow, thou shalt deny me thrice" (St. Matthew 26:31, 33, 34).

We are on dangerous ground when we begin to assume that we are superior in our spiritual relationship in the Lord. The Apostle Peter felt that everybody may fail and not measure up, but it will never happen to him. Others have voiced that same opinion. In the Old Testament Elijah was running for his life, as Jezebel was determined to put the prophet to death. Elijah was in need of rest and food. Satan tries to take advantage of our weaknesses, and tries us at such times. In I Kings this man of God prayed, "It is enough; now, O Lord, take away my life; for I am not better than my fathers." Then he said, "I, even I only am left; and they seek my life to take it away." But God informs Elijah, "Yet I have left me seven thousand in Israel, all the knees which have not bowed unto Baal, and every mouth which hath not kissed him" (19:4, 10, 18).

From these accounts and other incidences we readily see that all of us are still on probation and we must walk humbly and softly trusting the merits of the atonement Christ provided that we may gain that "Crown of righteousness" (II Timothy 4:8).

These truths reinforce the similar message found in Galatians 6:1. "Brethren, if a man be overtaken in a fault, ye which are spiritual, restore such a one in the spirit of meekness; considering thyself, lest thou be tempted." We should always remember the words of Jesus Christ, "And what I say unto you I say unto all, Watch" (St. Mark 13:37).

Is there hope for one who has been defeated in battle? Man may have given up on your case, but God has not. Our only hope is found in looking to Jesus Christ as the Israelites looked to the brazen serpent in the wilderness when bitten by snakes and they lived. Jesus used this account to look to Him as the one and only means to be forgiven and cleansed from sin. Listen to the account: "And as Moses lifted up the serpent in the wilderness, even so must the Son of man be lifted up: That whosoever believeth in Him should not perish, but have eternal life. For God so loved the world, that He gave His only begotten son, that whosoever believeth in Him should not perish, but have everlasting life. For God sent not His Son into the world to condemn the world; but that the world through Him might be saved" (St. John 3:14-17).

The contrite, brokenhearted backslider must be dealt with in a gentle manner. They are already down and discouraged. The last thing one in this condition needs is harsh and rough treatment. Note how Jesus responded to Peter's thrice betrayal. Our Master simply looked at his backslidden disciple and it broke the apostle's heart and Peter started to weep his way back to reinstatement in the family circle of believers.

Notice further Christ's approach in order to restore the fallen. Jesus saw what was going to take place in Peter's life and had a plan to meet his need. First He warned Peter of the approaching danger but assured him he had his Master's prayers. "And the Lord said, Simon, Simon, behold, Satan hath desired to have you that he may sift you as wheat: But I have prayed for thee, that thy faith fail not" (Luke 22:31-32). It is comforting to remember that Jesus Christ is also praying that our faith will not fail. "It is Christ that died, yea rather, that is risen again, who is even at the right hand of God, who also maketh intercession for us" (Romans 8:34).

In the High Priestly prayer of Jesus as found in St. John 17 we are assured that our Savior not only prayed for the disciples of that day, but for all succeeding generations. Listen to the Master's own words. "Neither pray I for these alone, but for them also which shall believe on Me through their word; That they may all be one; as Thou, Father, art in me, and I in thee, that they also may be one in us: that the world may believe that thou hast sent me" (St. John 17:20-21). Notwithstanding all the provision Christ provided, yet Peter went down in defeat. Jesus did not scold and rail on Peter, but simply looked at him, and it broke the apostle's heart, leading him to repentance. "And Peter remembered the word of Jesus, which said unto him, Before the cock crow, thou shalt deny me thrice. And he went out and wept bitterly" (St. Matthew 26:75).

We must be very careful in assisting the fallen and our approach in the restoration of the backslider. Jude admonishes us in verses 22 and 23, "And of some have compassion, making a difference. And others save with fear, pulling them out of the fire." The tender, disappointed, but loving look of his Master was enough to cause Peter to leave the crowd and seek solitude where he might be restored, and again take up his cross and follow his Lord. Peter took the sure route to recovery for God's word informs us that, "For godly sorrow worketh repentance to salvation not to be repented of: but the sorrow of the world worketh death" (II Corinthians 7:10).

The approach of Christ is always redemptive. We notice how Christ sought to restore the churches that had lost ground as found in Chapter 2 and 3 of Revelation. He would first encourage them by pointing out something good they still were doing. The fallen are already discouraged and if one can find something good to say it will encourage them to try again. I remember as a very young person going to my pastor for spiritual help. His advice made an indelible impression on my mind, for although I am ninety-one years old I still remember his good advice to me. He said, "Keep all the religion you have and get more." In essence that is what Jesus told the churches in Revelations.

This is still the approach of our Savior. Listen to our Lord's message in St. Matthew 12:20: "A bruised reed shall He not break, and smoking flax shall He not quench, till He send forth judgment unto victory." The reed is a tender and fragile plant at its best, but you can only imagine how much weaker when bruised. Jesus uses truth that is reinforced by saying He will not put out the flickering light of the lamp that is about to go out. Some of us still remember using the coal oil lamps, and how the wick had to be trimmed in order to get it to burn brightly again. The bottom line is that our Savior is doing His best to restore those who have fallen.

Such stories as the prodigal son and the lost sheep illustrate this truth. "How think ye? If a man have a hundred sheep, and one of them be gone astray, doth he not leave the ninety and nine, and goeth into the mountains, and seeketh that which is gone astray. And if so be that he find it, verily I say unto you, he rejoiceth more of that sheep, than of the ninety and nine which went not astray" (St. Matthew 18:12, 13).

When the prodigal son came to himself and decided to repent, he was received by his father with opened arms. Listen to his plan as he made preparation to return home. "I will arise and go to my father, and will say unto him, Father, I have sinned against heaven and before thee, and am no more worthy to be called thy son; make me as one of thy hired servants. And he arose, and came to his father. But when he was yet a great way off, his father saw him, and had compassion, and ran, and fell on his neck, and kissed him. And the son said unto him, father, I have sinned against heaven, and in thy sight, and am no more worthy to be called thy son. But the father said to his servants, Bring forth the best robe and put it on him; and put a ring on his hand, and shoes on his feet: And bring hither the fatted calf, and kill it; and let us eat, and be merry: For this my son was dead, and is alive again; and he was lost, and is found. And they began to be merry" (St. Luke 15:18-24).

There is an old saying, that goes something like this: "The bird with a broken or clipped wing will never fly as high again." That can never be said of the Apostle Peter, for he flew even higher. What made the difference? I answer by saying the same thing that makes the difference in any one of us, and that is the Upper Room experience, where he tarried for the baptism of the Holy Spirit. Pentecost cured Peter and it will make the difference as to whether we live a victorious life or a mediocre life of defeat.

Did Peter rise higher after his restoration to the favor of God? I would say so, for the apostle preached one simple sermon and had about 3,000 converts. Allow Luke to relate the account. "Then they that gladly received his word were baptized: and the same day there were added unto them about 3,000 souls" (Acts 2:41).

Yes, heaven and earth unite to celebrate one lost soul who returns to his Father's house. Jesus says, "I say unto you, that likewise joy shall be in heaven over one sinner that repenteth, more then over ninety and nine just persons, which need no repentance" (St. Luke 15:7).

We see by these Scriptures there is recovery for all who come as Peter did and can still bear fruit bringing the lost to Jesus.

Again, remember the Scripture already quoted. "For I know the thoughts that I think toward you, saith the Lord, thoughts of peace, and not of evil, to give you an expected end. Then shall ye call upon me, and ye shall go and pray unto me, and I will hearken unto you. And ye shall seek me, and find me, when ye shall search for me, with all your heart: and I will be found of you, saith the Lord" (Jeremiah 29:11-14).

2
KING DAVID: Viewing the Forbidden

"And it came to pass, after the year was expired, at the time when kings go forth to battle, that David sent Joab, and his servants with him, and all Israel, and they destroyed the children of Ammon, and besieged Rabbah. But David tarried still at Jerusalem. And it came to pass in an evening tide, that David arose from off his bed, and walked upon the roof of the king's house: and from the roof he saw a woman washing herself; and the woman was very beautiful to look upon. And David sent and inquired after the woman. And one said, Is not this Bathsheba the daughter of Eliam, the wife of Uriah the Hittite? And David sent messengers, and took her; and she came in unto him, and he lay with her for she was purified from her uncleanness: and she returned to her house. And the woman conceived, and sent and told David, and said, I am with child." —II Samuel 11:1-5.

"Have mercy upon me, O God, according to Thy loving kindness: according unto the multitude of Thy tender mercies blot out my transgressions. Wash me throughly from mine iniquity, and cleanse me from my sin... Purge me with hyssop, and I shall be clean, wash me, and I shall be whiter than snow... Restore unto me the joy of Thy salvation; and uphold me with thy free Spirit. Then will I teach transgressors thy ways; and sinners shall be converted unto thee." —Psalm 51:1-3, 7, 12-13.

ON THE OCCASION of Abner's death King David lamented that tragedy, saying to his servants, "Know ye not that there is a prince and a great man fallen this day in Israel?" (II Samuel 3:38) These words were spoken by David after General Joab had taken the life of an innocent man. The physical death of Abner was a grievous act of injustice resulting in the physical death of a great man. But it cannot be compared to the spiritual death that took place in the heart of King David when he willfully planned and executed that design by shedding innocent blood, bringing heartache to the nation with the ripples of that act spreading out in all directions, even to this present day.

The death of Abner was temporary from which there would be recovery, but David's death was spiritual and eternal unless a genuine repentance would take place. Here we view a great man of God who had fallen from lofty heights to the lowest depths.

Recently a plane was lost with over 200 people aboard. An intensive search has been taking place with various countries united in order to find the plane and hopefully survivors, or at least part of the wreckage in order to see what went wrong that such a disaster would happen, and make necessary corrections so as to avoid such calamity in the future of aviation.

If it is necessary to find the cause of a problem with aircraft in order to help passengers to make a safe landing in the future, then how much more should we study what happened in the lives of these biblical characters to cause their downfall. In fact God's Word exhorts us that we should study individuals so that we can avoid such evil things as some of them practiced and fell from the grace of God. Note I Corinthians 10:5-6: "But with many of them God was not well pleased: for they were overthrown in the wilderness. Now these things were our examples, to the intent we should not lust after evil things, as they also lusted."

The question may be asked by some sincere people, "Was King David really a follower of God?" Let us see what God's Word says. When God was looking for a man with a pure heart to replace King Saul, who failed to obey God's orders, He found none other than David. He met the standard God required in order to rule His people Israel. In I Samuel 13:14 we read, "The Lord hath sought Him a man after his own heart, and the Lord hath commanded him to be captain over His people." This statement is enough and settles the issue that David was a man whose character was above reproach, since his heart was in harmony with the heart of his Creator. Yet, in the crucial test this great man of God failed.

Many who are strong have been defeated. Even Satan was one of the greatest angels in heaven. This trio consisted of Gabriel, Michael, and Satan. God has given every intelligent being a free will. Like Pilate we have to decide what we will do with Jesus Christ who loves us so much that "while we were yet sinners, Christ died for us" (Romans 5:8). Satan was powerful and so influential that not only did he fall but took one third of the angels down to the pit. These all once were beautiful angelic beings praising God. But as strong as they were, they fell from their high position and descended to the depths. God never created demons as such, for they were all formed as angels but chose to leave a paradise. When one rejects Christ, the only alternative to heaven is to a region that our Savior speaks of as

"Where their worm dieth not, and the fire is not quenched" (Mark 9:48).

Since so many strong individuals have gone down in defeat we can readily see the need of this warning found in I Corinthians 10:12, "Wherefore let him that thinketh he standeth take heed lest he fall.

Now, let us look at David's life as we view his calling, his rise to power, his downfall, and his recovery.

David was a goodly young man serving God with all his heart. God directed Samuel to bypass all of his brothers in selecting a replacement for King Saul. We read in I Samuel 16:12 that "…He was ruddy, and withal of a beautiful countenance, and goodly to look to…" *Ruddy* in part means he had a healthy countenance. This was a fringe benefit. Up to this time David had lived a clean, pure life and like Daniel and the three Hebrew children who refused to eat and drink what the king had assigned for their meals. "Their countenances appeared fair and fatter in flesh than all the children which did eat the portion of the king's meat" (Daniel 1:15).

While Godly living improves one's appearance, God was looking for a deeper beauty. In selecting a king God told Samuel to "Look not on his countenance, or on the height of his stature; because I have refused him: for the Lord seeth not as man seeth; for man looketh on the outward appearance, but the Lord looketh on the heart" (I Samuel 16:17). Evidently no one thought of David even as a candidate in the process of selecting a king, for he was tending the sheep as his older brothers passed by Samuel in the process of selecting one to become king. But God saw the potential in this young man, the bottom line being his degree of love for God and the building of His kingdom.

David had done exploits before he became king. He killed a bear, a lion, and a giant without weapons of war. What ammunition he had consisted of a sling shot and a few stones from the brook. What made him invulnerable was his total dependence upon God. Listen as he testifies to Goliath the giant before their encounter. "Then said David to the Philistine, Thou comest to me with a sword, and with a spear, and with a shield: but I come to thee in the name of the Lord of hosts, the God of the armies of Israel, whom thou hast defied" (I Samuel 17:45).

Because of his dependence on God, David was gaining and compounding his strength to fight the battle involving the building of God's Kingdom and his people, Israel. "And the women answered one another as they played, and said, Saul hath slain his thousands, and David his ten thousands" (I Samuel 18:7).

Eventually David was crowned King. He now was in a position where he was invested with power and authority. King David's influence was widespread. It is a strategy of Satan to not only devour an individual but slay and destroy his followers. The Apostle Paul realized this truth as he writes, "Lest Satan should get an advantage of us: for we are not ignorant of his devices" (II Corinthians 2:11).

The Bible speaks of "the destruction that waste at noonday" (Psalm 91:6). There are many who have successfully overcome the storms of youth, only to go down during the heat of noonday.

The enemy attacks us at the point where he is most likely to succeed. The assault often comes after we have experienced a great outpouring of the Holy Spirit, as it happened to our Savior after His baptism. We read, "And Jesus, when He was baptized, went up straightway out of the water: and, lo, the heavens were opened unto Him, and he saw the Spirit of God descending like a dove, and lighting upon Him: And lo a voice from heaven saying, This is my beloved Son, in whom I am well pleased" (St. Matthew 3:16-17). Then immediately we read, "Then was Jesus led up of the Spirit into the wilderness to be tempted of the devil" (St. Matthew 4:1). The enemy repeatedly takes advantage of us when we are physically exhausted, as he did with the prophet Elijah, or when one becomes overconfident, as in the life of Peter, who was convicted by the crowing of a cock.

What brought about David's downfall? As we will see later it stemmed from the spiritual condition of his heart, but there were other things that contributed to place the king in jeopardy. In II Samuel 11:1 we find this particular incident in the life of David that took place during the time "when kings go forth to battle," but in the same verse we read that instead of going to battle in his own person, "that David sent Joab, and his servants with him, and all Israel." Then still in that verse God's Word tells us, "But David tarried still at Jerusalem."

In Chapter 10 of II Samuel we read of a mighty victory David won over the Syrians, then the next chapter tells of his awful spiritual defeat he experienced in his moral life. David neglected duty, and had time that he idled away in sin. The old adage is true that "an idle mind is the devil's workshop." It is always dangerous to be idle. Jesus took his disciples apart for rest and relaxation, but it was in order that they would be recharged for the next call to duty. David not only wasted his time, but spent it in an unlawful pursuit. Any pleasure experienced in yielding to sin is very short-lived. God's Word proclaims, "Bread of deceit is sweet to a man; but afterwards his mouth shall be filled with gravel" (Proverbs 20:1).

Years ago I heard a fine young man testify concerning how a Christian can have a good time, and feel good about it the day following. In other words, it doesn't leave a bad taste in the mouth as found in the proverb just quoted. Moses chose "to suffer affliction with the people of God than to enjoy the pleasures of sin for a season; Esteeming the reproach of Christ greater riches than the treasures in Egypt: for he had respect unto the recompense of the reward" (Hebrews 11:25-26). This great man of God was willing to forego any temporary pleasure that might be found in disobedience to God, for he viewed life on earth from the perspective of eternity. In contrast Esau sold his birthright losing the blessing God had in store for him if he had only waited on God's timing.

In following this wise choice that Moses took, one finds that it yields temporary enjoyments as well as eternal happiness. Paul in writing to young Timothy reminds him that, "Godliness is profitable unto all things, having promise of the life that now is, and of that which is to come" (I Timothy 4:8).

Satan now had his bait set and in order, as in the temptation of our first parents. We read that "when the woman saw that the tree was good for food, and that it was pleasant to the eyes, and a tree to be desired to make wise, she took of the fruit thereof, and did eat, and gave also unto her husband with her; and he did eat, and the eyes of them both were opened" (Genesis 3:3-7).

King David followed this same course as he swallowed not only the bait but also the hook. As in the first fall, David's eyes were opened. He sees his terrible loss. If only he had followed Job's example who had "made a covenant with mine eyes; why then should I think upon a maid?" (Job 3:1)

Now the wages of sin are in view. Tragedy upon tragedy follow. "At last it biteth like a serpent, and stingeth like an adder" (Proverbs 23:32). The king's first plan was, like our first parents, to hide. He tried to deceive the nation by a subtle plan to make it appear that Uriah was the father of the child conceived by this sin. This action backfired on him, and David had this loyal, godly man, Uriah, placed in a very dangerous position in the war so he would die, and King David could take his wife. This second plan succeeded, but only temporarily, as only the blood of Christ can cover sin, for Jesus says, "For there is nothing covered, neither hid, that shall not be known" (Luke 12:2).

How true this came to pass in the following events that

took place in the life of David. "Thus saith the Lord, Behold, I will raise up evil against thee out of thine own house, and I will take thy wives before thine eyes, and give them unto thy neighbor, and he shall lie with thy wives in the sight of this sun. For thou didst it secretly: but I will do this thing before all Israel and before the sun" (II Samuel 12:11, 12). David lived to see his sins reproduced in the lives of his children and many consequences of his sins.

But the Prophet Nathan came to David and told the parable of the rich man (II Samuel 12) who spared his flock and slaughtered the poor man's lamb. We find that David's heart broke and he came clean with God and man, and he repents as found in Psalm 51. He no longer hides, but with his heart crushed he prays, "For I acknowledge my transgression and my sin is ever before me" (Psalms 51:3). He wanted relief from a guilty conscience and to be restored to that intimate relationship he formerly had with God. Is this possible?

Let us see what God says. "My little children, these things write I unto you, that ye sin not. And if any man sin, we have an advocate with the Father, Jesus Christ the righteous: and He is the propitiation for our sins: and not for ours only, but also for the sins of the whole world" (I John 2:1-2). Praise God!

God has planned and made it possible for us by His atonement to live above sin in a sinful world, but has also made provision as in the scripture just quoted for our restoration if we should sin. I heard Dr. Purkiser once say it is like having a spare tire in your automobile; you don't plan on using it, but it is good to have if you should have a flat tire. The stories found in St. Luke 15 of the Lost Sheep, the Lost Coin, and the Prodigal proves God's willingness to receive those who sincerely repent.

David's steps to being restored were as follows in Psalm 51:

1. His dependence on the mercy of God - verse 1

2. His desire to go to a deeper experience - verse 2

3. Confession of his sins - verse 3

4. While many suffered because of his sin, he realized all sin is ultimately against God. Joseph knew this in his temptations and said, "How can I do this great wickedness and sin against God?" (Genesis 39:9)

5. Verses 5, 6, 7, David gets to the heart of the matter and sees that his sin sprouted from an unclean heart.

In verse 5 he mentions he was born with a sinful nature, and then proceeds to pray not only for forgiveness, but for a clean heart. Jesus said, "For out of the heart proceed evil thoughts, murders, adulteries, fornications, thefts, false witnesses, blasphemies: These are the things which defile a man" (Matthew 15:19-20).

Many are constantly hacking at the branches of the tree and never touching the root. Years ago we lived in a parsonage where a bank behind the house was infested with poison ivy. I was determined to clear the ground of the poisonous weed. It took time but I stayed with the endeavor and it was well worth all my efforts as I destroyed the roots.

We find as the disciples tarried in the upper room at Pentecost for the baptism of the Holy Spirit, (Acts 2), something happened that made such a radical change that the world looked on in wonder and said, "These that have turned the world upside down are come hither also" (Acts 17:6).

As you study the lives of the disciples before Acts 2, contrasted with their ministry after the upper room experience, one can readily see the fruits of that experience, since they were cleansed from inbred sin. In a pre-Pentecostal Age, by faith King David laid hold on the promise and his life was changed. In Psalm 51 David prayed for a clean heart and restoration of his joy he had lost. We can be sure God answered his prayer, for we read in I Thessalonians 5:23-24, "And the very God of peace sanctify you wholly; and I pray God your whole spirit and soul and body be preserved blameless unto the coming of our Lord Jesus Christ. Faithful is He that calleth you, who also will do it."

So if you should be so unfortunate as to have fallen from grace, take courage, as God is no respecter of persons and what our Lord did in reclaiming King David, He will do for you. Amen! "And I will restore to you the years that the locust hath eaten, the canker worm, and the caterpillar, and the palmerworm" (Joel 2:25). What God did for His people in that far off age, He will do for us in this present dispensation of grace. Jesus says, "him that cometh to me I will in no wise cast out" (St. John 6:37).

3
MIRIAM: Jealousy

"And Miriam and Aaron spoke against Moses because of the Ethiopian woman whom he had married: for he had married an Ethiopian woman. And they said, Hath the Lord indeed spoken only by Moses? Hath He not spoken also by us? And the Lord heard it... And the anger of the Lord was kindled against them; and he departed. And the cloud departed from off the tabernacle; and, behold, Miriam became leprous, white as snow: and Aaron looked upon Miriam, and behold she was leprous. And Aaron said unto Moses, I beseech thee, lay not the sin upon us, wherein we have done foolishly, and wherein we have sinned... And Moses cried unto the Lord, saying, Heal her now, O God, I beseech thee... And Miriam was shut out from the camp seven days: and the people journeyed not till Miriam was brought in again." —Numbers 12:1-2, 9-11, 13, 15.

MOSES, AARON AND MIRIAM completed a trio that God mightily used in the building of His kingdom in those days. Although, the youngest, Moses was chosen by God to be the leader. Aaron was the priest and Miriam was called to be a Prophetess. We read, "And Miriam the prophetess, the sister of Aaron, took a timbrel in her hand; and all the women went out after her with timbrels and with dances. And Miriam answered them, Sing ye to the Lord, for He hath triumphed gloriously; the horse and his rider hath He thrown into the sea" (Exodus 15:20-21).

Evidently Miriam was a born leader, called to be a prophetess, even in those days when women were held in very low esteem. After the crossing of the Red Sea she led a large choir of women in singing praise to God for their victory over the Egyptians. Her influence was great and she was placed by God in a high position of honor. Satan turns his most powerful weapons on such.

Now there is a turn of events. There may have been a simmering coal of jealousy in her heart as she thought of the Egyptian woman that Moses chose to marry. There was nothing wrong morally with that union; it was not as if he had married a Canaanite (Deuteronomy 7:14).

Often when one has an unsolved problem of sin in his or her own life, an attempt by the convicted one will be to transfer it to an innocent person in order to find relief. Again listen to the account: "Hath the Lord indeed spoken only by Moses? Hath He not spoken also by us?" (Numbers 12:2) Miriam was no longer content, but a most miserable person. She no longer had a song in her heart as in former days when she sang and celebrated freedom from Egyptian bondage. Sin also causes physical problems. Sleepless nights, fear, indigestion, and a host of other conditions may be the result of an unclean spiritual heart condition.

Christian leaders may continue for a while to carry on their work by running on momentum, but eventually the lack will appear.

When the children of Israel were held in captivity at

Babylon their conquerors required them to sing. They said, "Sing us one of the songs of Zion" (Psalm 137:3). They didn't ask for a popular or worldly song, but they wanted to hear from God. But God's people could only answer by saying, "How shall we sing the Lord's song in a strange land?" (Psalm 137:4) No doubt there were no problems with their vocal cords, but their sin caused them to be in bondage at Babylon, which is synonymous of one living in Satan's territory.

Here was an opportunity to win a heathen nation to the God of Israel, but this opening was lost, because God's people were not spiritually alive themselves. Jesus asked, "Can the blind lead the blind? Shall they not both fall into the ditch?" (Luke 6:39) That is why David prayed, "Restore unto me the joy of Thy salvation; and uphold me with Thy free Spirit. Then will I teach transgressors thy ways; and sinners shall be converted unto Thee" (Psalms 51:12-13). For the same reason Jesus commanded His disciples to "tarry ye in the city of Jerusalem, until ye be endued with power from on high" (Luke 24:49).

In earlier days they use to talk about a ring in a testimony. What that meant was it had the unction of the Holy Spirit. Jesus said, "for without me ye can do nothing" (St. John 15:5) When I was a boy we had an interurban railroad connecting my home city, Lancaster, Ohio with our State Capital, Columbus, Ohio. The single coach was powered by a dangerous electrical charged third rail. When coming to a road crossing for safety the rail had to be separated, and the interurban would coast until it was reconnected on the other side of the road. During that brief time all power was lost and darkness took place.

Even so when Jesus Christ is rejected, the result is darkness, for we are not a vacuum. When Judas Iscariot betrayed Christ, the scripture says, "He then having received the sop went immediately out: and it was night" (St. John 13:30).

Miriam briefly experienced darkness in her soul. She had given way to a sin of the spirit, jealousy, which can be more deadly than sins of the flesh. Why? Sins of the spirit are not always easily detected immediately. One may appear as a respectable person and harbor a grudge, unforgiving spirit, murder, adultery, etc; and still go through the motions of serving God. "For man looketh on the outward appearance, but the Lord looketh on the heart" (I Samuel 16:7).

It was when the sin was confessed (Numbers 12:11-12) that Miriam was on the way to full recovery. She was a precious and a valuable asset in God's plan of redemption through the nation of Israel. We find that the whole conquest of Canaan came to a standstill until Miriam was healed.

Although Moses was the one targeted in this sin of jealousy, yet he was forgiving even as later on Christ taught us to "Love your enemies, bless them that curse you, do good to them that hate you, and pray for them which despitefully use you, and persecute you; That ye may be the children of your Father which is in heaven" (St. Matthew 5:44-45). Listen to the prayer of Moses for his sister, Miriam. "And Moses cried unto the Lord, saying, Heal her now, O God, I beseech thee" (Numbers 12:13).

God answered his prayer. God healed her, but she was chastened for her good (Hebrews 12:1-14) and consequently "shut out from the camp seven days" (Numbers 12:14). The people didn't take their journey until Miriam was taken back and completely restored to the camp.

This great leader and woman of God did not despair in her backslidden state, but did what was necessary to be reinstated in God's army and again she served God. She then lived and died in the faith, her death being recorded in Numbers 20:1.

If you have failed God, he will restore you if you come back as Aaron and Miriam humbly approached the mercy seat. "For the Son of man is come to save that which was lost" (St. Matthew 18:11).

4
JONAH: Disobedience

"Now the word of the Lord came unto Jonah the son
of Amitar saying, Arise go to Nineveh, that great city,
and cry against it; for their wickedness is come up before me. But Jonah rose up to flee unto Tarshish from
the presence of the Lord, and went down to Joppa; and
he found a ship going to Tarshish: so he paid the fare
thereof, and went down into it, to go with them unto
Tarshish from the presence of the Lord. But the Lord
sent out a great wind into the sea, and there was a
mighty tempest in the sea, so that the ship was like to
be broken... Then they said unto him, Tell us, we pray
thee, for whose cause this evil is upon us; What is thine
occupation? And whence comest thou? What is thy
country? And of what people art thou? And he said
unto them, I am an Hebrew; and I fear the Lord, the
God of heaven, which hath made the sea and the dry
land... And he said unto them, Take me up, and cast
me forth into the sea; so shall the sea be calm unto
you: for I know that for my sake this great tempest is
upon you. Nevertheless the men rowed hard to bring
it to the land; but they could not: for the sea wrought,

and was tempestuous against them... So they took up Jonah, and cast him forth into the sea: and the sea ceased from her raging... Now the Lord had prepared a great fish to swallow up Jonah. And Jonah was in the belly of the fish three days and three nights... Then Jonah prayed unto the LORD his God out of the fish's belly... And the LORD spake unto the fish, and it vomited out Jonah upon the dry land." —Jonah 1:1-4, 8-9, 12-13, 15, 17, 2:1, 10

SOME TREAT THIS inspired account of Jonah's experience as a myth or an allegory. I well remember when I was a young man, how a minister engaged me in conversation and said the stories in the Old Testament are myths. Jesus didn't teach them as myths. Jesus taught the Book of Jonah as a historical fact illustrating His death and resurrection by it. We read, "An evil and adulterous generation seeketh after a sign; and there shall no sign be given to it, but the sign of the prophet Jonas: For as Jonas was three days in the whale's belly; so shall the Son of man be three days and three nights in the heart of the earth" (Matthew 12:39, 40). Our Savior spoke with authority and that should forever settle the issue.

Our emphasis as we study this portion of God's Word should not be placed on the miracle of the prepared fish that swallowed Jonah, but on the love of God for all human kind as well as His love for his lower creation. The concluding verse of Chapter 4:11 pretty well summarizes the thrust of the Book. The Lord says, "And should not I spare Nineveh, that great city, where are more than six score thousand persons that cannot discern between their right hand and their left hand; and also much cattle?

Jonah was not a false prophet, but a true and genuine messenger called of God to proclaim His Word, and to warn sinners of judgment to come. God's inspired Word substantiates the fact that Jonah was no counterfeit prophet as we read of God's estimate of this prophet in II Kings 14:25. "He restored the coast of Israel from the entering of Hamath unto the sea of the plain, according to the word of the Lord God of Israel, which he spake by the hand of his servant Jonah."

So we see he was a clean vessel to channel God's message to Israel. Also, Jonah passed the test used to distinguish a true prophet of God from the false. The examination was simply to wait and see if the prophet's message would come to pass. The prophet Jonah was a truthful and powerful preacher. He knew in his own heart that his messages were from God and would be fulfilled, but he also knew that the God he served is merciful and ready to forgive when sinners truly repent. The prophet preached and God so powerfully used the message that revival broke out and the entire city was delivered from the threatened judgment.

One would think the prophet would rejoice as no doubt all heaven was rejoicing for Jesus says, "Likewise, I say unto you, there is joy in the presence of the angels of God over one sinner that repenteth" (St. Luke 15:10). If there is that much joy among the heavenly hosts when one lost soul is born again, we can only imagine the jubilee and celebration that took place around the Throne when more than 120,000 heathen prayed and put their trust in the true and living God of Israel (Jonah 4:11).

Jonah, as we already noted, was a good man, a genuine prophet and honored by God, but it appears that briefly he gave way to the devourer of souls when he was more interested in his reputation as a prophet than the message God called him to deliver. We read, "But it displeased Jonah exceedingly, and he was very angry. And he prayed unto the Lord, and said, I pray thee, O Lord, was not this my saying, when I was yet in my country? Therefore I fled unto Tarshish: for I knew that Thou art a gracious God, and merciful, slow to anger, and of great kindness, and repentest thee of the evil. Therefore now, O Lord, take, I beseech thee, my life from me; for it is better for me to die than to live" (Jonah 4:1-3).

Jonah found out, as all find sooner or later, that the path of disobedience is hedged with thorns. He was called to be the minister for a citywide evangelistic campaign to be held at Nineveh. But Jonah rejected the opportunity God had opened in order to evangelize a large city of 120,000 never-dying souls for which he considered an easier way. No doubt the Prophet reasoned as King David did who said, "Oh that I had wings like a dove! For then would I fly away, and be at rest" (Psalm 55:6). The Psalmist found that flight was not the answer to his problems but God would meet his need, for later in the same Psalm, David exhorts, "Cast thy burden upon the Lord, and he shall sustain thee: he shall never suffer the righteous to be moved" (Psalm 55:22).

The safest place we can be is in the center of God's will. I once heard of a young lady who felt a call to be a missionary, but her father blocked her way to fulfill her mission. The result as I remember was that she stayed in this country and was murdered. This girl's father found out as Jonah did that God's will is the safest course we can follow in this life.

God loved Jonah as He loves all of us. In fact He loves us so much that He finds it is necessary for Him to discipline us for our eternal good when He sees we are headed for destruction. In Hebrews 12:5-6 we read, "And ye have forgotten the exhortation which speaketh unto you as unto children, My son, despise not thou the chastening of the Lord, nor faint when thou art rebuked of him: for whom the Lord loveth he chasteneth, and scourgeth the every son whom he receiveth."

Why should we bear chastisements in such a manner? We find the answer in verse 11 of the same chapter which reads, "Now no chastening for the present seemeth to be joyous, but grievous: nevertheless afterward it yielded the peaceable fruit of righteousness unto them which are exercised thereby."

There are times when God uses extraordinary means in order to get the attention of those who do not heed the drawing power of the Holy Spirit, but desire to follow their own pernicious ways which leads to death. In order to avoid this tragedy, God reluctantly allows some seemingly disaster to take place.

In the Book of Lamentations 3:31, 33 we read, "For the Lord will not cast off forever: But though he cause grief, yet will he have compassion according to the multitude of His mercies. For he doth not afflict willingly nor grieve the children of men." God is so reluctant to resort to this method of permitting men to suffer in order to draw them to him that he speaks of it as his strange work. Isaiah writes, "For the Lord shall rise up as in mount Perazim, he shall be wroth as in the valley of Gibeon, that he may do his work, his strange work. And bring to pass his act, his strange act" (Isaiah 28:21).

But God had not forgotten the prophet although it appears it took one of his strange acts to bring Jonah back to the Good Shepherd who was in search of his one lost sheep. This prophet was deeply humbled as he still was able to pray although he was now inside the fish. The account says, "Then Jonah prayed unto the Lord his God out of the fish's belly, And said, I cried by reason of mine affliction unto the Lord, and he heard me; out of the belly of hell cried I, and thou heardest my voice" (Jonah 2:12).

According to the above scripture God heard Jonah's prayer, and now after escaping from solitary confinement, he is ready again for his ministry at Nineveh. One notices the prophet was not released from his call of duty. But he was given a second chance. How similar the calls! Jonah 1:2, "Arise, go to Nineveh." The second call reveals the same summons, "Arise, go unto Nineveh" (Jonah 3:2). After repentance takes place, inevitably our faith will again be tested at the point where one failed. So it was with Jonah!

The prophet Jonah still had a problem as you notice when reading the last chapter, but God tenderly helped him to cope with his weaknesses.

The message delivered in the Book of Jonah reveals God's love for all his creation, and none need to despair, although they have failed, if genuine repentance takes place.

Potentially God is the Savior of all men, but conditionally of those who repent, for God's Word reads, "For therefore we both labour and suffer reproach, because we trust in the living God, who is the Savior of all men, specially of those that believe" (I Timothy 4:10). God longs to restore the backslider. In the last chapter of the Bible the message is "Whosoever will, let him take the water of life freely" (Revelation 22:17). Will you accept the invitation? Our Lord and Savior Jesus Christ is waiting with outstretched arms to receive you.

5
JACOB: Deception

"And Isaac his father said unto him, Who art thou? And he said, I am thy son, thy firstborn Esau... And he said, Thy brother came with subtilty, and hath taken away thy blessing. And he said, is not he rightly named Jacob? For he hath supplanted me these two times: he took away my birthright; and behold, now he hath taken away my blessing." —Genesis 27: 32, 35-36

IN ORDER TO GET the whole picture of this account, one must read the 27th chapter of Genesis in its entirety. This scripture along with others leads us to the conclusion that deception was the besetting sin of Jacob.

Jacob, along with many others during the intervening years, had the false opinion that life could be lived successfully by practicing deception. Such deluded people have never read God's Word, or did not heed the message they heard as found in Numbers 32:23, "Be sure your sin will find you out." Jacob, along with all who follow this path of deception, found this way only leads to heartache and despair. In Proverbs 20:17 we read, "Bread of deception is sweet to a man; but afterwards his mouth shall be filled with gravel."

There was a time in my ministry when I had to find employment to supplement my salary. I well remember when applying for this work how the one interviewing me said, "We will have to go a little underhanded." I would rather starve to death than to supply my need by such a sinful approach. Later in life Jacob had a drastic change in his life for good, but in his earlier days he was going underhanded in his attempt to achieve.

What caused such a twist in his nature that propelled him to have such a passion to follow this sin of deception. It was the same that King David found as recorded in Psalm 51:5. "Behold, I was shapen in iniquity; and in sin did my mother conceive me." Sin manifests itself differently, but it all comes from the same root. In other words we are all born with a sinful nature.

What influences caused these smoldering coals to spring forth so violently into action? We must look at the patriarch's early home life. His parents were good people coming from the seed of Abraham who was known as a friend of God, but both had a common flaw in their hearts which was deception.

Earlier in this chapter we find Jacob's mother, Rebekah, devising a deceptive plan to accomplish her evil purpose by deceiving her aging husband, Isaac, by way of taking advantage of his failing eyesight. Not only was Rebekah sinning against God and her husband, but she was leading her son to follow her example in order to execute this diabolical act, instead of using her God given mother influence to guide her son in the straight and narrow way which leads to life. We read, "Now therefore, my son, obey my voice according to that which I command thee" (Genesis 27:8).

Isaac, Jacob's father, was a good man and worthy to be followed as a role model, but there was one isolated act when he lied and said his wife was his sister in order to save his own life. The accounts reads, "And Isaac dwelt in Gerar: and the men of the place asked him of his wife; and he said, She is my sister: for he feared to say, She is my wife; lest, said he, the men of the place would kill me for Rebekah; Because she was fair to look upon" (Genesis 26:67).

Here we see a double negative influence for deception was exerted on Jacob by both parents by example and precept. Also we note how sin unchecked can follow generations. Abraham lived so close to God, that he was known as God's friend (II Chronicles 20:7). Yet, when under pressure he failed and gave way to the sin of deception, by the agency of his wife, Sarah. Like his son Isaac, in an attempt to spare his life, Abraham told Sarah to "Say, I pray thee, thou art my sister; that it may be well with me for thy sake; and my soul shall live because of thee" (Genesis 12:13).

Abraham's plan of deception failed, but he tried the same plot in order to deceive Abimelech. "And Abraham said of Sarah his wife, She is my sister: and Abimelech king of Gerar sent, and took Sarah" (Genesis 20:3). Again his evil design was thwarted when the truth was made known to Abimelech by means of a dream (Genesis 20:3).

When Abimelech protested to Abraham and declared his innocence in this matter, the patriarch having then been confronted as to his motive for committing such a crime, answered by saying, "Because I thought, Surely the fear of God is not in this place; and they will slay me for my wife's sake. And yet indeed she is my sister; she is the daughter of my father, but not the daughter of my mother; and she became my wife" (Genesis 20:11-12).

Anything one does with the desire to deceive is deception. Half truths told with such an end in view constitute a lie, and according to God's Word such will be lost unless genuine repentance takes place for we read, "and all liars shall have their part in the lake which burneth with fire and brimstone: which is the second death" (Revelation 21:8).

I am taking liberty to digress a bit concerning Jacob, for there is a practical truth for all generations that needs to be emphasized lest we unwittingly follow the footsteps of Jacob.

I have observed over a period of many years how this sin of deception has been committed, and seemingly without any prick of conscience.

There are those who deceive by using a phone to record their lie. The message says, "I can't answer now, but leave your number and I will call you," when all the time they were waiting to see who called in order to answer or hang up the receiver.

I know of one who did shoddy work for a lady, then said she will never know it, for her room is dark. But listen to what Jesus says: "There is nothing covered, that shall not be revealed; neither hid, that shall not be known. Therefore whatsoever ye have spoken in darkness shall be heard in the light; and that which ye have spoken in the ear in closets shall be proclaimed upon the housetops" (St. Luke 12:23).

Perhaps, there are those who "talk down" a product when making a purchase only to "talk it up" when selling it so as to make a larger profit, and then call it good business. But God has a better definition for such practice. In Jeremiah 22:13 we read, "Woe unto him that buildeth his house by unrighteousness, and his chambers by wrong, that useth his neighbor's service without wages, and giveth him not for his work."

The basic sin is still deception. My first pastorate consisted of very few people with very little support. I well remember of a Christian man who hired me to cut corn. He never told me what my wages would be; consequently I was never paid. I want to think it was just an oversight on his part, but we must be careful in all our relationships lest we come up short on Judgment Day.

There finally comes a time when one must stop running from God, and accept responsibility for his or her own actions, regardless of all the contributing factors that may have entered as a part of the crisis. Jacob had come to this fork in his journey alone.

Jacob had now come to a place where he needed help and needed it desperately. He like Balaam, could no longer run from God, but had to face up to the harvest he was now reaping from past decisions. Jacob would soon meet his brother Esau whom he had tricked out of both his birthright and blessing. Fear and uncertainty grasped the heart of Jacob. So he devised a plan to pacify his brother be giving him a large gift of his livestock. Then Jacob sent messengers to deliver the scheme (Genesis 32:3). "And the messengers returned to Jacob, saying, We came to thy brother Esau, and also he cometh to meet thee, and four hundred men with him. Then Jacob was greatly afraid and distressed" (Genesis 32:6-7). It would be a "head on" collision.

But God was ready to give Jacob a second chance and a new start. Jacob saw his problem, but he also saw the solution to his perplexing situation. First we see his problem as recorded in Genesis 33:7. "And Jacob lifted up his eyes, and looked, and, behold Esau came, and with him four hundred men."

Perhaps Jacob was now thinking of how he had deceived his twin brother and of how good it would be if only he could go back and now be able to resist the temptation. Years ago one of our General Superintendents of our denomination, said that he would give his right hand if he had not failed in the past, or similar words.

He did not elaborate. He is now in heaven where even our scars are removed, for he was a godly man, saved and sanctified wholly.

None us can change the decisions we made in the past, which Satan uses in order to discourage us and weaken us in our spiritual warfare. We can't make the needed change, but I know One who can. In Jeremiah 13:23 we read, "Can the Ethiopian change his skin, or the leopard his spots? Then may ye also do good, that are accustomed to do evil." But thanks be to God that what can not be done in the realm of nature can be accomplished spiritually through the blood of Jesus Christ.

When the Apostle Paul was in despair as he was plagued by what he called "the body of this death," he found the only solution to his perplexity in his distress, would be to trust in the Lord Jesus Christ for cleansing. Here he was referring to an ancient form of capital punishment, as a corpse was tied to a criminal until the decomposition of the dead would eventually take the life of the living. St. Paul uses this metaphor to explain how unchecked inbred sin finally leads to spiritual death. Notice the conclusion the apostle arrives at in Romans 7:24-25: "O wretched man that I am. Who shall deliver me from the body of this death? I thank God through Jesus Christ our Lord."

Before Jacob faced his brother Esau, a radical change took place in Jacob. He did what he could, humanly speaking, in order to save at least part of his family and possessions. He divided his company into two bands, so if Esau would strike one company the other would be left (Genesis 32:7-8). But that, however, was not good enough. Jacob needed assurance from God and soul rest.

Jacob now needs time alone with God. The account reads, "And he rose up that night, and took his two wives and his two women servants, and his eleven sons, and passed over the ford Jabbok. And he took them, and sent them over the brook, and sent over that he had. And Jacob was left alone; and there wrestled a man with him until the break of day" (Genesis 32:22-24).

When one is in earnest as Jacob was, Satan will do all in his power to hinder his prayer, but Jacob would not flinch. He said, "I will not let thee go, except thou bless me" (Genesis 32:26). It was about daybreak when Jacob prayed through and "struck fire."

We read, "And he said unto him, What is thy name? And he said, Jacob. And he said, Thy name shall be called no more Jacob [heel grasper], but Israel [prince]: for as a prince hast thou power with God and with men, and hast prevailed" (Genesis 32:27-28).

What God did for Jacob, He will do for you and give you a new start if you truly repent as Jacob did, "For there is no respect of persons with God" (Romans 2:11). Man may never forgive you, but God will, for we read, "As the east is from the west, so far hath he removed our transgressions from us" (Psalms 103:12). "What shall we then say to these things? If God be for us, who can be against us?" (Romans 8:31)

6
Thomas: Unbelief

"Then the same day at evening, being the first day of the week, when the doors were shut where the disciples were assembled for fear of the Jews, came Jesus and stood in the midst, and saith unto them, Peace be unto you. And when He had so said, He shewed unto them his hands and his side. Then were the disciples glad, when they saw the Lord… But Thomas, one of the twelve, called Didymus, was not with them when Jesus came. The other disciples therefore said unto him, We have seen the Lord. But he said unto them, Except I shall see in his hands the prints of the nails, and put my finger into the print of the nails, and thrust my hand into his side, I will not believe. And after eight days again his disciples were within, and Thomas with them: then came Jesus, the doors being shut, and stood in the midst, and said, Peace be unto you. Then saith He to Thomas, Reach hither thy finger, and behold my hands; and reach hither thy hand, and thrust it into my side: and be not faithless, but believing. And Thomas answered and said unto him, My Lord and my God. Jesus saith unto him, Thomas, because thou hast seen me, thou hast believed: blessed ore they that have not seen and yet have believed." —St. John 20:19-20, 24-29)

"Take heed, brethren, lest there be in any of you an evil heart of unbelief, in departing from the living God." —Hebrews 3:12)

"But without faith it is impossible to please him: for he that cometh to God must believe that he is, and that he is a rewarder of them that diligently seek him." —Hebrews 11:6

THIS DISCIPLE IS USUALLY referred to as "Doubting Thomas." We must remember that Thomas "was not with the other disciples when Jesus came" (St. John 20:24). One wonders what the response of the other disciples would have been if they had not been present when Jesus made His first appearance to his disciples. It is easy to judge others when you have not walked in their shoes.

But to the everlasting credit of Thomas, he wanted to base his faith on a solid foundation of certainties and not on the sinking sands of doubt. There are other biblical characters who followed the same route as Thomas in their quest for certainty. "Gideon said unto God, If thou wilt save Israel by mine hand, as thou hast said, Behold, I will put a fleece of wool in the floor; and if the dew be on the fleece only, and it be dry upon all the earth beside, then shall I know that thou wilt save Israel by mine hand, as said. And it was so, for he rose up early on the morrow, and thrust the fleece together, and wringed the dew out of the fleece, a bowl full of water. And Gideon said unto God, Let not thine anger be hot against me, and I will speak but this once: let me prove, I pray thee, but this once with the fleece; let it now be dry only upon the fleece, and upon all the ground let there be dew. And God did so that night: for it was dry upon the fleece only, and there was dew on all the ground" (Judges 6:36-40).

Also, when King Hezekiah was informed by the Prophet Isaiah of his imminent death, the good king made it a matter of prayer. The Word of God says, "Then he turned his face to the wall, and prayed unto the Lord, saying, I beseech thee, O Lord, remember now how I have walked before thee in truth and with a perfect heart, and have done that which is good in thy sight. And Hezekiah wept sore. And it came to pass, afore Isaiah was gone out into the middle court, that the word of the Lord came to him, saying, Turn again, and tell Hezekiah the captain of my people, Thus saith the Lord, the God of David thy father, I have heard thy prayer, I have seen thy tears: behold. I will heal thee: on the third day thou shalt go ye unto the house of the Lord… And Hezekiah said unto Isaiah, What shall be the sign that the Lord will heal me, and that I shall go up in the house of the Lord the third day? And Isaiah said, This sign shalt thou have of the Lord, that the Lord will do the thing that he hath spoken: shall the shadow go forward ten degrees, or go back ten degrees? And Hezekiah answered, It is a light thing for the shadow to go down ten degrees: nay, but let the shadow return backward ten degrees. And Isaiah the prophet cried unto the Lord: and he brought the shadow ten degrees backward, by which it had gone down in the dial of Ahaz" (II Kings 20:2-5, 8-11).

In these instances, God had spoken and his message was clear, yet these men wanted further assurance. At this point is where the element of unbelief enters, and if not checked may lead one down the road to final apostasy. This is one of the wiles of the devil. Mother Eve fell by reasoning with Satan. At times the enemy will even tempt us to doubt the word of God or misinterpret it as he did in the Garden of Eden and later used the same tactic in tempting our Lord and Savior, but failed. We should never put God to the test in an attempt to get further evidence of his will after he has revealed it to us. Balaam did this after he was certain of God's will and his life ended in disaster. Our faith rests solidly on the eternal Word of God which is a sure road map for our journey to heaven. Jesus says, "Heaven and earth shall pass away, but my words shall not pass away" (St. Matthew 24:35).

The other disciples saw Jesus and believed, but Thomas wanted even more proof. He said, "Except I shall see in his hands the print of the nails, and put my finger into the print of the nails, and thrust my hand into his side, I will not believe" (St. John 20:25). He was adamant that he would not believe unless he had the privilege of proving that Jesus Christ had arisen from the tomb both by the sense of sight and touch.

In the Christian life we live by faith and not feeling. It has been said that Isaac went by feeling and was deceived. In both the Old and New Testament we are exhorted to live by faith. "But the just shall live by his faith" (Habakkuk 2:4). "For therein is the righteousness of God revealed from faith to faith, as it is written: The just shall live by faith" (Romans 1:17).

It was over eighty years ago that God for Christ's sake saved my soul, and I have learned the secret to a victorious Christian life is to make sure all is clear with our Savior, then continue to live for God regardless of feeling. There are times in my devotions when it seems like I am nearing the third heaven, but at other times if I went by feeling I would think my prayer didn't get through. I also know at times we are accomplishing the most at these times.

Daniel was a man of spotless character, yet there was a time when he was resisted by Satan in his communion with God. We read in Daniel 10:12-14, "Then said he unto me, Fear not, Daniel: for from the first day that thou didst set thine heart to understand, and to chasten thyself before thy God, thy words were heard, and I am come for thy word. But the prince of the kingdom of Persia withstood me one and twenty days: but, lo, Michael, one of the chief princes, came to help me; and I remained there with the kings of Persia, Now I am come to make thee understand."

So we see the necessity of faith in the Christian life. Abram "believed in the Lord; and he counted it to him for righteousness" (Genesis 15:6). In the context we find God told Abram that his heir would be "he that shall come forth out of thine own bowels" (Genesis 15:4). Abram already believed in the Lord, but the faith spoken of in this passage was the faith Abram exhibited by simply believing what God promised in the absence of any sign or extra proof. In the Book of James God tells us, "Abraham believed God, and it was imputed unto him for righteousness: and he was called the friend of God" (James 2:23).

Jesus says, "Ye are my friends, if ye do whatsoever I command you" (St. John 15:14). Therefore, we see friendship with God is the reward for our faith and obedience.

Personally, I do not feel that Thomas broke his relationship with our Savior in this scriptural account of his failure to believe until he had extra proof.

Perhaps there are times when it would be in order for many of us to pray as the father of the son who was bound by the dumb spirit, as he prayed to Jesus, "and said with tears, Lord, I believe; help thou mine unbelief" (St. Mark 9:24). God never turns a deaf ear to honesty. It is good to lay out before God our weaknesses and confess we can not cope with the situation. That is what this father did and Jesus answered and healed this son as we find the full account in St. Mark 9:14-30.

God does not cast us off as a reprobate at the first suggestion from Satan to doubt, but restores our faith as Jesus did for Peter when the apostle's faith failed when he took his eyes off Jesus and fastened them on the boisterous waves that threatened him as he walked on the water. St. Matthew 14:30-31 records, "But when he saw the wind boisterous, he was afraid; and beginning to sink, he cried, saying, Lord, save me. And immediately Jesus stretched forth his hand, and caught him, and said unto him, O thou of little faith, wherefore didst thou doubt?" Whenever we take our eyes off of Jesus and gaze at our surroundings we will, as in the case of Peter, begin to sink. I had a lady in one of my pastorates that failed to keep spiritual victory, because she had her eyes focused on people. Jesus found it necessary to correct Peter for this same problem. Jesus had just told Peter about the kind of death that the apostle would experience, and Peter turned about and saw "the disciple whom Jesus loved following. Peter seeing him saith to Jesus, Lord, and what shall this man do? Jesus saith unto him, If I will that he tarry till I come, what is that to thee? follow thou me" (St. John 21:20-22). We are not responsible for the actions of others in the sense of acting as their judge. "Who art thou that judgest another? (James 4:12) It is our duty to walk in the light God sheds on our pathway.

What practical lessons do we glean as we study the life and experiences of Thomas? The first and uppermost truth is, that the best way to overcome the temptation to doubt is to cultivate and increase our faith according to God's Word. Jesus taught the apostles this truth as recorded in the Gospel of St. Luke 17:3-5, which reads, "If thy brother trespass against thee, rebuke him; and if he repent, forgive him. And if he trespasses against thee seven times in a day, and seven times in a day turn again to thee, saying, I repent; thou shalt forgive him, And the apostles said unto the Lord, Increase our faith." Yes, that is our need— an increase of faith.

In the physical realm we can fight disease by attempting to avoid germs, etc., and we should surely do that, but a more effective approach is to practice good health habits until our immune system is strengthened to resist the approaching bacteria. The latter method is the biblical way to conquer unbelief and doubt by practicing the spiritual truths of God's Word which in turn, will lead to a healthy, victorious faith.

After describing the awful depraved condition of men and "angels which kept not their first estate" (Jude verse 6); the inspired writer gave God's people instruction as how to overcome in a hostile and sinful world. Jude writes, "But ye, beloved, building up yourselves on your most holy faith, praying in the Holy Ghost, Keep yourselves in the love of God, looking for the mercy of our Lord Jesus Christ unto eternal life" (Jude 20-21). So, we see there are things which we can do in order to increase our faith.

While we are saved by faith, "Not of good works, lest any man should boast," (Ephesians 2:9). Yet, James cites how faith is followed by works resulting in the perfecting of faith as in the account of Abraham by faith offering up his son Isaac. "Seest thou how faith wrought with his works, and by works was faith made perfect?" (James 2:22)

Also in order to increase our faith we need to read God's Word as a love letter from heaven, which indeed it is. Take time and let God speak through His Word. The Psalmist says, "Thy word have I hid in my heart, that I might not sin against thee" (Psalm 119:11). Jesus Christ resisted all the temptations of Satan by quoting scripture, and we have the same promises and access to the Word of God as our Savior had.

We need to memorize God's Word and become familiar with it that we can immediately detect when it is misquoted. Years ago, a lady in my aunt's Sunday School class thought she was quoting from the Bible when she said, "You know that scripture, that all roads lead to Rome." This is just one example of many.

Thomas arose from doubt to a strong faith. His testimony is brief but to the point as found in St. John 20:28,

"And Thomas answered and said unto him, My Lord and my God."

May God help us all to mount up to the realms of a living active faith. Amen.

7
MOSES: Presumption

"And all the congregation of the children of Israel journeyed from the wilderness of Sin, after their journeys,
according to the commandment of the Lord, and
pitched in Rephidim: and there was no water for the
people to drink. Wherefore the people did chide with
Moses, and said, Give us water that we may drink. And
Moses said unto them, Why chide ye with me? Wherefore do ye tempt the Lord? And the people thirsted
there for water; and the people murmured against
Moses, and said, Wherefore is this that thou hast
brought us up out of Egypt, to kill us and our children
and our cattle with thirst? And Moses cried unto the
Lord, saying, What shall I do unto this people? They
be almost ready to stone me. And the Lord said unto
Moses, Go on before the people, and take with thee of
the elders of Israel; and thy rod, wherewith thou
smotest the river, take in thy hand, and go. Behold, I
will stand before thee upon the rock in Horeb; and
thou shalt smite the rock, and there shall come water
out of it, that the people may drink. And Moses did so
in the sight of the elders of Israel." —Exodus 17:1-6

"Then came the children of Israel, even the whole congregation, into the desert of Zin in the first month: and
the people abode in Kadesh; and Miriam died there,
and was buried there. And there was no water for the
congregation: and they gathered themselves together
against Moses and against Aaron… And the Lord spake
unto Moses, saying, Take the rod, and gather thou the
assembly together, thou and Aaron thy brother, and
speak ye unto the rock before their eyes, and it shall
give forth his water, and thou shalt bring forth to them
water out of the rock: so thou shalt give the congregation and their beasts drink… And Moses lifted up his
hand, and with his rod he smote the rock twice: and
the water came out abundantly, and the congregation
drank, and their beasts also. And the Lord spake unto
Moses and Aaron, Because ye believed me not, to sanctify me in the eyes of the children of Israel, therefore
ye shall not bring this congregation into the land which
I have given them." —Numbers 20:1-2, 7-8, 11-12

HERE WE HAVE two scriptural accounts of God
miraculously meeting the needs of his people
in a dry and thirsty land. The same miracle
of supplying water from the rock took place on two
different occasions. Moses obeyed God's instruction
recorded in Exodus, but failed when the same need
arose in a different vicinity.

In the first miracle God told Moses to take his staff and
smite the rock in order to supply their need for water. He
explicitly obeyed the Lord and was not only blessed with
abundance of water, but maintained God's approval.

In the second miracle as recorded in the twentieth chapter of Numbers, God told Moses to speak to the rock in
order to supply water for the congregation and the beasts.
Instead of speaking to the rock, he smote the rock twice,
contrary to God's instructions.

This act of disobedience kept Moses from leading the people into the Promised Land. Perhaps there are those who wonder why a seemingly small act like this would bring such a severe penalty. We must remember that it is not the size or nature of the test, but our obedience to God is what counts. When man was placed on probation in the Garden of Eden, his test of allegiance to his Creator was very simple. God had provided an ample supply of food for our first parents, but restricted them from using the fruit from "the tree of the knowledge of good and evil," evidently as a test of their loyalty.

God did not create us as robots, but gave us freedom to exercise our liberty by choosing or rejecting our Lord. In those ancient days, God gave his people Israel, the choice of serving false gods, or the true and living God. After explaining to the people what was involved in the resolution, Joshua, their leader, cried out, "And if it seem evil unto you to serve the Lord, choose you this day whom ye will serve; whether the gods which your fathers served that were on the other side of the flood, or the gods of the Amorites, in whose land ye dwell: but as for me and my house, we will serve the Lord" (Joshua 24:15). Also, the Hebrew slave after serving his master for six years had the privilege of choosing to leave as a free man or because of love for his master, his wife and his children, he could decide to stay and serve him forever (see Exodus 21:16). He then would be known as a love slave.

Our love and obedience to God must remain firm and steadfast for the entire period of our probation on earth. Jesus says, "But he that shall endure unto the end, the same shall be saved" (Matthew 24:13).

Moses obeyed God at Rephidim, and struck the rock one time as God had commanded, but as so often happens, defeat can follow victory. Men begin to trust their ability and no longer rely on God. Jesus makes it clear in St. John 15:5, "For without me ye can do nothing." King David said,

"The Lord is the strength of my life" (Psalm 27:1).

We find many examples both in the Bible and in our day of those who have followed this course leading to their destruction and downfall. King Asa of Judah was forced to fight against superior forces, and felt his inadequacy to defeat such military might. He felt his complete dependence upon trusting God for victory, and he was not disappointed.

We read, "And Asa cried unto the Lord his God, and said, Lord, it is nothing with thee to help, whether with many, or with them that hath no power: help us, O Lord our God; for we rest on thee, and in thy name we go against this multitude. O Lord, thou art our God; let not man prevail against thee. So the Lord smote the Ethiopians before Asa and before Judah; and the Ethiopians fled" (II Chronicles 14:11-12).

Later when Judah was threatened by Israel, King Asa hired the Syrians to defend them instead of trusting God as in the previous war. "And at that time Hanani the Seer came to Asa, King of Judah, and said unto him, Because thou hast relied on the king of Syria, and not relied on the Lord thy God, therefore is the host of the king of Syria escaped out of thine hand. Were not the Ethiopians and the Lubims a huge host, with very many chariots and horsemen? Yet, because thou didst rely on the Lord, he delivered them into thine hand" (II Chronicles 16:7-8).

Solomon was mightily used of God in his younger days, when he felt his need of God and depended on the Lord. But he turned from God and served idols, thus alienating himself from the true and living God.

These and many other illustrations show us the necessity of heeding the Word of God as we read, "Wherefore let him that thinketh he standeth take heed lest he fall" (I Corinthians 10:12).

Moses who served God so faithfully, and warned his followers of the danger involved by disobeying the commands of God; fell into the same trap, thus forfeiting his privilege of entering Canaan land. "And the Lord spake unto Moses and Aaron, Because ye believed me not, to sanctify me in the eyes of the children of Israel, therefore ye shall not bring this congregation into the land which I have given them" (Numbers 20:12).

But the story does not end here. Was there any hope left for Moses and those who fall? Thank God there is or many of us would have fallen into despair. If you, the reader, should have been so unfortunate as to have fallen from grace, do you not now hear God wooing you in the following scripture, "My little children, these things write I unto you, that ye sin not. And if any man sin, we have an advocate [attorney] with the Father, Jesus Christ the righteous: And he is the propitiation for our sins: and not for ours only, but also for the sins of the whole world" (I John 2:1-2).

"If we confess our sins, he is faithful and just to forgive us our sins, and to cleanse us from all unrighteousness" (I John 1:9).

Did Moses ever enter Canaan? He did not enter during his earthly pilgrimage, but many years later we find Moses met Jesus on the Mount of Transfiguration along with Peter, James, and John. We read the account in St. Matthew 17:1-3, "And after six days Jesus taketh Peter, James, and John his brother, and bringeth them up into an high mountain apart, and was transfigured before them: and his face did shine as the sun, and his raiment was white as the light. And, behold, there appeared unto them Moses and Elias talking with him." With such a beatific vision and experience I feel sure Moses was now satisfied of reaching his goal of entering the Promised Land. Moses was temporally down, but like the Prodigal Son he arose and went back to his Father.

Some people will not forgive, and Satan will continue to accuse one of past forgiven sins in order to weaken and discourage, but "if God be for us, who can be against us?" (Romans 8:31) David testified, "As far as the east is from the west, so far hath he removed our transgressions from us" (Psalms 103:12). "For the son of man is come to save that which was lost" (St. Matthew 18:11).

The last chapter and message in the Bible includes a universal call for all to come. "And the Spirit and the bride say, come. And let him that is athirst come. And whosoever will, let him take the water of life freely" (Revelation 22:17).

This invitation is extended to you, my brother and sister. "Thanks be unto God for his unspeakable gift" (II Corinthians 9:15).

8

JOHN MARK: Terminated Mission

"And some days after Paul said unto Barnabas, Let us
go again and visit our brethren in every city where we
have preached the word of the Lord, and see how they
do. And Barnabas determined to take with them John,
whose surname was Mark. But Paul thought not good
to take him with them, who departed from them from
Pamphylia, and went not with them to the work. And
the contention was so sharp between them, that they
departed asunder one from another: and so Barnabas
took Mark, and sailed unto Cyprus; And Paul chose
Silas, and departed, being recommended by the brethren unto the grace of God." —Acts 15:36-40

"Take Mark, and bring him with thee: for he is profitable to me for the ministry." —II Timothy 4:11

JOHN MARK WAS AN OUTSTANDING soldier of the Cross
and contributed much to the establishment of the
early church. His influence continues to this day
and it will continue in generations to come. Like
Timothy, Mark had a godly heritage. His mother's

home in Jerusalem was one of the meeting places for the early church. He was a close companion of the Apostle Peter, and when the apostle was miraculously delivered out of prison by the angel of the Lord (Acts 12:1) Peter immediately went to the home of Mark's mother where a great prayer meeting was in progress.

This close intimacy that Peter had with Mark's family permitted John Mark to hear firsthand from the apostle the mighty works, and life of our Lord Jesus Christ. The Bible does not state whether or not Mark was an immediate follower of Jesus. Tradition is not united in answering this question. However, God inspired John Mark under Divine inspiration to write one of our sixty-six books of the Holy Bible. If he was not an immediate follower of Christ, he could have received much information from the Apostle Peter who calls Mark his son.

In this scripture (Acts 15:36), we find Paul suggesting to Barnabas that they return to the places where they had preached and see how the new converts were doing. Perhaps many lose out, because of our failure to follow up new converts. Barnabas agreed to go on this second mission, but he wanted to take Mark who had left them on their pioneer mission.

Both Paul and Barnabas were good men, but men of strong will. Barnabas was willing to give John a second chance, but Paul didn't think he should go after having left them on their first mission. So they parted. "And the contention was so sharp between them, that they departed asunder one from the other: and so Barnabas took Mark, and sailed unto Cyprus; and Paul chose Silas, and departed, being recommended by the brethren unto the grace of God" (Acts 15:39-40).

We should not conclude that Mark backslid when "he departed from them from Pamphylia, and went not with them to the work" (Acts 15:38). We do not know the reason he decided to leave, for the scripture merely states the fact that he left. Evidently Paul must have thought there was no sufficient reason to have excused him from this present ministry.

But there may have been circumstances of which we are not aware. We as Christians should put the best interpretation possible on the conduct of others, so long as we do not compromise the plain teaching of God's Word. For example as pastors, we sometimes, in order to reach the lost, find it necessary to go where smoke fills the premises. As a result our clothes become saturated with smoke. In making the next call, it would be easy for those being called on to feel sure their pastor took up the harmful habit of smoking. Even worse, they could spread the rumor with much spiritual damage as a result.

So we do not know what caused John Mark to not finish his work. However, there is a lesson for all. Sins of omission are as deadly as sins of commission. In James 4:17 we read, "Therefore to him that knoweth to do good, and doeth it not, to him it is sin."

At the Judgment Jesus will say, "Then shall he say also unto them on the left hand, depart from me, ye cursed, into everlasting fire, prepared for the devil and his angels: For I was an hungered, and ye gave me no meat: I was thirsty, and ye gave me no drink: I was a stranger, and ye took me not in: naked, and ye clothed me not: sick and in prison, and ye visited me not. Then they shall also answer him, saying, Lord, when saw we thee an hungred, or athirst, or a stranger, or naked, or sick, or in prison, and did not minister unto thee? Then shall he answer them saying, verily I say unto you, inasmuch as ye did it not to one of the least of these, ye did it not to me. And these shall go away into everlasting punishment: but the righteous into life eternal" (St. Matthew 25:31-46).

The Apostle Paul realized the danger of not fulfilling our

known duty as God's people. Listen to the apostle: "Woe is unto me, if I preach not the gospel!"(I Corinthians 9:16) You may not be called to preach, but then, there is a ministry for all as we observe the spiritual and physical hunger the world over.

If John Mark failed, he surely came back stronger in his love for God and souls. In fact, Paul indirectly admits that he was wrong and Barnabas was right, for later he writes, "Take Mark, and bring him with thee: for he is profitable to me for the ministry" (II Timothy 4:11). Yes, John Mark was surely profitable. He not only was used to write the gospel that bears his name, but in that day, the Apostle Paul now sees in this servant of God what he had failed to see earlier.

Reader, have you failed in neglecting the work God has planned for your life? If so, take up the cross you laid down. Repent and then tarry for your personal Pentecost, and no longer stand idle, but enter our Master's vineyard, for there is a great harvest, but few laborers. Listen to the Master's call for workers: "But when he saw the multitudes, he was moved with compassion on them, because they fainted, and were scattered abroad, as sheep having no shepherd. Then saith he unto his disciples, The harvest truly is plenteous, but the labourers are few; Pray ye therefore the Lord of the harvest, that he will send forth labourers into his harvest" (St. Matthew 9:36-38).

9
Two Prodigal Sons: Sins of the Flesh and Sins of the Spirit

"And he said, a certain man had two sons: and the younger of them said to his father, Father, give me the portion of goods that falleth to me. And he divided unto them his living. And not many days after the younger son gathered all together, and took his journey into a far country, and there wasted his substance with riotous living. And when he had spent all, there arose a mighty famine in that land; and he began to be in want. And he went and joined himself to a citizen of that country; and he sent him into his fields to feed his swine. And he would fain have filled his belly with the husks that the swine did eat: and no man gave unto him. And when he came to himself, he said, How many hired servants of my fathers have bread enough and to spare, and I perish with hunger! I will arise and go to my father, and will say unto him, Father, I have sinned against heaven and before thee, And am no more worthy to be called thy son: make me as one of thy hired servants. And he arose and came to his father. But when he was yet a great way off, his father saw him, and had compassion, and ran, and fell on his neck, and kissed him. And the son said unto him, Father, I have sinned against heaven, and in thy sight, and am no more worthy to be called thy son. But the father said to his servants, Bring forth the best robe, and put it on him; and put a ring on his hand, and shoes on his feet: and bring hither the fatted calf, and kill it; and let us eat, and be merry: For this my son was dead, and is alive again; he was lost, and is found. And they began to be merry. Now his elder son was in the field: and as he came and drew nigh to the house, he heard music and dancing. And he called one of the servants, and asked what these things meant. And he said unto him, thy brother is come; and thy father hath killed the fatted calf, because he hath received him safe and sound. And he was angry, and would not go in: therefore came his father out, and intreated him. And he answering said to his father, Lo, these many years do I serve thee, neither transgressed I at any time thy commandment: and yet thou never gavest me a kid: that I might make merry with my friends: But as soon as this thy son was come, which hath devoured thy living with harlots, thou hast killed for him the fatted calf. And he said unto him, Son, thou art ever with me, and all that I have is thine. It was meet that we should make merry, and be glad: for this thy brother was dead, and is alive again; and was lost, and is found." —St. Luke 15:11-32

THIS SCRIPTURAL ACCOUNT is one of the three parables Jesus gave us to show the love, compassion, and willingness of our Savior to forgive and restore the backslider when he humbles himself and truly repents. Jesus spoke these truths in parables. A parable corresponds pretty much to an illustration. The common and natural sights and experiences of life are used to illustrate moral and spiritual truth. Although this is a parable and gives no certain individual's name, yet it does not diminish the value of the truths taught, for there are many who take the same route as the sons in this parable.

Our Lord uses three parables to teach us his desire to forgive. They are: 1.The Lost Sheep, 2. The Lost Coin, and 3. The Lost Son. We will limit this discussion to the third parable, the Lost Son, which is commonly referred to as the Prodigal Son. Although, the main thrust of this parable is to teach the Pharisees and scribes a lesson concerning their attitude toward lost sinners, for whom Christ died to save.

The introduction to these parables reads, "Then drew near unto him all the publicans and sinners for to hear him. And the Pharisees and scribes murmured saying, This man receiveth sinners, and eateth with them" (St. Luke 15:1-2). So it is the attitude of the elder son that corresponds to that of the Pharisees and scribes. The younger son fell by way of fleshly lusts while the elder son yielded by sins of the spirit which can be more difficult to detect, for it does not always readily appear on the surface. However, all sin eventually shows and comes to light unless forgiven. In Genesis 4:5 we read, "But unto Cain and to his offering he had not respect. And Cain was very wroth, and his countenance fell" (also in Isaiah 39).

"The shew of their countenance doth witness against them; and they declare their sin as Sodom, they hide it not." Both sons were in need of God's forgiveness.

Today, August 9, 2014, as I write sin is rampant in our world. Things are rapidly coming to pass just as God declared in His Word, which points to Jesus Christ's Second Coming. Sin is on the increase and laws are now being passed that protect and promote sin. There has been hideous sin ever since the fall, but now sin is practiced without any shame.

There were those in the days of the prophet Jeremiah who acted in a similar manner. We read, "Were they ashamed when they had committed abomination? Nay, they were not at all ashamed, neither could they blush" (Jeremiah 6:15). Is there a cure for sin today? There are not many remedies, but only one which is all sufficient. Here it is: "If we confess our sins, he is faithful and just to forgive us our sins, and to cleanse us from all unrighteousness" (I John 1:7).

Let us now look at the course the younger prodigal son took in order to be restored to his father. First, we need to see what caused his fall into sin. He had become discontented with life as he knew it at home. He may have reasoned that his home life was too monotonous and routine as he did his chores on the farm. Life is pretty much routine for most of us, but the prodigal failed to see what God's people know; how serving God, and doing what work we do as a sacrament unto the Lord brings satisfaction. It did in the life of the Apostle Paul as he writes, "For I have learned, in whatsoever state I am, therewith to be content" (Philippians 4:11).

The Prodigal's discontentment led him to request his inheritance, which was unwisely granted to him by his father. He thought worldly sinful pleasure would satisfy the severe vacuum he experienced in the depth of his spirit. Jesus told the woman at the well, "Whosoever drinketh of this water shall thirst again: But whosoever drinketh of the water that I shall give him shall never thirst; but the water that I shall give him shall be in him a well of water springing up into everlasting life" (St. John 4:13-14).

The young man had made his decision and now, sin had been conceived as his will had united with the tempter. Satan wastes no time in leading his victim into greater bondage. St. Luke 15:13 tells us that "not many days after the younger son gathered all together, and took his journey into a far country, and there wasted his substance with riotous living."

After having wallowed in the mire and pit of sin, he finally came to himself; he was able to see that sin has a payday. We read in Proverbs 20:17, "Bread of deceit is sweet to a man; but afterwards his mouth shall be filled with gravel." Years ago, I heard a young man say that what he liked about serving the Lord was the way you feel the next day. One can have a good time as a Christian, and have a clear conscience afterward. Moses knew this truth to be a fact as he chose to serve God rather "than to enjoy the pleasures of sin for a season" (Hebrews 11:25).

This lost son now realizes how happy and good his life used to be at home, contrasted to his existence as he lived among the hogs. So, he decides on a plan to make a change. He said, "I will arise and go to my father, and will say unto him, Father, I have sinned against heaven, and before thee, And am no more worthy to be called thy son: make me as one of thy hired servants" (St. Luke 15:18-19).

This account reminds one of the times when the Syrians "warred against Israel" (II Kings 6:8). Also, "there was a great famine" (II Kings 6:25). As a result of the famine, death by starvation was imminent. There were four lepers who devised a plan we read about in II Kings 7:3-4, "And there were four leprous men at the entering in of the gate: and they said one to another, Why sit we here until we die? If we say, We will enter into the city, then the famine is in the city, and we shall die there: and if we sit still here, we die also. Now therefore come and let us fall unto the host of the Syrians: if they save us alive, we shall live; and if they kill us, we shall but die."

Their plan was rewarded, for when they approached the Syrian camp they found that "the Lord had made the host of the Syrians to hear a noise of horses, even the noise of a great host" (II Kings 7:6). Consequently in their haste to flee from the supposed enemy, the Syrians left an abundance of food behind, which was evidently enough to meet all the starving people of Israel.

These lepers were willing to fall into the hands of the enemy in their despair hoping the enemy would save their lives. Dear reader, if you have fallen into sin, don't sit there any longer, but do like the prodigal as he said, "I will arise and go to my father" (St. Luke 15:18).

You will not be falling into the arms of an enemy, but into the embrace of the true and living God who welcomes you and who will reinstate you, not as a hired servant but as his son. Like the elder son who was not willing to forgive, so you may find such today, but God says, "Bring forth the best robe, and put it on him; and put a ring on his hand, and shoes on his feet: And bring hither the fatted calf, and kill it; and let us eat, and be merry: For this my son was dead, and is alive again; he was lost, and is found. And they began to be merry" (St. Luke 15:22-24).

There may be some who read these lines who still have faith in Jesus Christ, but have failed so many times that they have lost faith in their ability to live the Christian life. Such people should remember it is Christ living in us and being filled with the Holy Spirit, which is the secret to living a victorious Christian life in a fallen world. The Apostle Paul writes, "I am crucified with Christ: nevertheless I live; yet not I, but Christ liveth in me: and the life which I now live in the flesh I live by the faith of the Son of God, who loved me, and gave himself for me" (Galatians 2:20).

Let us see how God restores those who have fallen by way of presumptuous sins being a willful transgression of a known law of God as in the case of King David. First, he must repent consisting of a godly sorrow along with confession. God's Word says, "For godly sorrow worketh repentance to salvation not to be repented of: but the sorrow of the world worketh death" (II Corinthian 7:10). King David truly repented of his sins, as recorded in Psalm 51, but he wanted God to take care of the underlying source of his problem.

The Bible speaks of sin and sins. Sins are the result of our personal choices for which we are responsible, but sin is what Theologians call original sin, with which we were born. David speaks of it in Psalm 51:6. "Behold, I was shapen in inquity; and in sin did my mother conceive me." He is not saying he was born as an illegitimate child, but that he was born with a nature that was contrary and not subject to the law of God (Romans 8:6-7).

We say a man is a sinner, but the Bible teaches that man commits sins, because his heart is unclean. Our Lord and Saviour Jesus Christ says, "But those things which proceed out of the mouth come forth from the heart; and they defile the man. For out of the heart proceed evil thoughts, murders, adulteries, fornications, thefts, false witness, blasphemies: These are the things which defile a man" (St. Matthew 15:18-20). David wanted a deeper experience with God, and he prayed, "Create in me a clean heart, O God, and renew a right spirit within me" (Psalm 51:10).

Last words are very important as we bid farewell to our relatives and friends. Jesus' last words after having completed his earthly mission was, "And, behold, I send the promise of my Father upon you: but tarry ye in the city of Jerusalem, until ye be endued with power from on high" (St. Luke 24:49). This, the disciples along with others did. Our Lord had assured the disciples that their names were written in heaven as noted in St. Luke 10:20: "Rejoice, because your names are written in heaven." Yet, Christ told his disciples there was a deeper experience which consisted of being filled with the Holy Spirit.

After Peter was baptized with the Holy Spirit he preached a simple message consisting mostly of quoting Old Testament prophecies, etc. He was now anointed and so filled with the Holy Spirit that about three thousand were converted and added to their number, which was probably more in one day than the combined ministry of Christ's followers produced in the three preceding years, while the Master was by their side. This is the need of the universal Church today and in all ages.

The Prodigal said, "I will arise and go to my Father" (St. Luke 15:18). If you have strayed from the Good Shepherd, then come as the Prodigal did, and I guarantee on the authority of God's Word you will be received into the arms of our loving Father. Come just as you are.

We find the last chapter in the Bible contains an invitation to come. "And the Spirit and the bride say, Come. And let him that heareth say, Come. And let him that is athirst come. And whosoever will let him take the water of life freely" (Revelation 22:17). May "the grace of the Lord Jesus Christ, and the love of God, and the communion of the Holy Ghost, be with you all. Amen" (II Corinthians 13:14).

10
How to Keep from Falling

"But ye, beloved, building up yourselves on your most holy faith, praying in the Holy Ghost, keep yourselves in the love of God, looking for the mercy of our Lord Jesus Christ unto eternal life." —Jude 20, 21

"I pray not that thou shouldest take them out of the world, but that thou shouldest keep them from the evil." —St. John 17:15

"Be not overcome of evil, but overcome evil with good." —Romans 12:21

IN THIS BRIEF LETTER Jude is writing "to them that are sanctified by God the Father, and preserved in Jesus Christ, and called" (Jude 1). Although these people were filled with the Holy Spirit, he warns them of the danger of falling from their faith by citing how angels who kept not their first estate fell (verse 6). Also Jude illustrates this truth by Old Testament examples of those who turned away from God through unbelief. No wonder we are exhorted in Hebrews 3:12-14 to "Take heed, brethren, lest there be in any of you an evil heart of unbelief, in departing from the living God. But exhort one another daily, while it is called Today; lest any of you be hardened through the deceitfulness of sin. For we are made partakers of Christ, if we hold the beginning of our confidence steadfast unto the end."

The inspired writer not only warns us of the dangers we face in a fallen world but shows us how to overcome and live a victorious holy life. We readily see the emphasis Jude places on the need of being on the offensive as we face our spiritual enemies. David did not wait for the giant to come to him, but ran to the giant and won the victory.

That is what the Apostle Paul proclaims when he wrote, "Be not overcome of evil, but overcome evil with good" (Romans 12:21). In the context, Romans 12:19-20, he gives us a practical illustration of offensive spiritual warfare. We overcome by returning good for evil. Jesus tells us to pray for our enemies and go the second mile. This approach works.

At the beginning of this chapter, St. John 17, the reader will note that our Lord Jesus Christ in His high priestly prayer prayed not to take us out of the world, but to keep us from the evil (St. John 17:15). Then in St. John 17:16 Jesus makes it clear as to their spiritual experience when He prayed, "They are not of the world, even as I am not of the world."

Yet our Savior realized they had a deeper need. He continues to pray, "Sanctify them through thy truth: thy word is truth" (St. John 17:17). It is true the word sanctify has two meanings as found in the Bible. To sanctify often means to set apart, as things in the Old Testament were set apart for holy use. But it is also used in speaking of entire sanctification or of being filled with the Holy Spirit, as it happened in Acts 2:4 and elsewhere. The Apostle Paul had this in mind, as he wrote in I Thessalonians, "And the very God of peace sanctify you wholly; and I pray God your spirit and soul and body be preserved blameless unto the coming of our Lord Jesus Christ" (I Thessalonians 5:22).

Again we look at the prayer of Christ found in St. John 17:19, which reads, "and for their sakes I sanctify myself, that they also might be sanctified through the truth." The word *sanctify* is used in both senses in this verse. Jesus is praying to be set apart for the purpose of shedding His blood as an atonement for sin in order that His disciples could be cleansed from sin.

This truth is explained in Hebrews 13:12. "Wherefore Jesus also, that he might sanctify the people with his own blood, suffered without the gate."

Pentecost was surely an answer to this prayer. I like the prayer following in verse 20 of this chapter, St. John 17: "Neither pray I for these alone, but for them also which shall believe on me through their word." That prayer includes you and me.

Even the Old Testament saints by faith saw a better spiritual experience then they at that time experienced. When Pentecost took place, the people who tarried in order to be filled with the Holy Spirit were so happy that those looking on "were all amazed and were in doubt, saying one to another, what meaneth this?" (Acts 2:12)

The Apostle Peter answers their question by quoting from the Old Testament prophet Joel, "But this is that which was spoken by the prophet Joel; And it shall come to pass in the last days, saith God, I will pour out of my Spirit upon all flesh: and your sons and daughters shall prophesy, and your young men shall see visions, and your old men shall dream dreams: and on my handmaidens I will pour out in those days of my Spirit; and they shall prophesy" (Acts 2:16-18).

God is waiting to meet your need. As a born again believer, have you stumbled so many times until you feel there is no use to try again? Don't give up. Come just as you are.

Make sure you are trusting Jesus Christ for forgiveness of personal committed sins, then with an unconditional surrender, pray for cleansing of your heart from what Theologians call original sin that we inherit from the fall. Here is a promise from God's Word to strengthen your faith. Jesus says, "If ye then being evil, know how to give good gifts, unto your children: how much more shall your heavenly Father give the Holy Spirit to them that ask him?" (St. Luke 11:13)

In closing this chapter on "How to Keep From Falling" we must remember there are some things we must do to grow and keep a healthy spiritual experience.

1. Feed on the Word of God. "As new born babes desire the milk of the word, that ye may grow thereby" (I Peter 2:2).

2. Regular prayer. "And he spoke a parable unto them to this end, that men ought always to pray, and not to faint" (St. Luke 18:1).

3. Attend a spiritual church. "Not forsaking the assembly of ourselves together, as the manner of some is; but exhorting one another: and so much the more as ye see the day approaching" (Hebrews 10:25).

4. Keep company with people of faith.

5. Meditate (not daydreaming). "But his delight is in the law of the Lord; and in his law doth he meditate day and night" (Psalm 1:2).

6. Good works. "Even so faith if it hath not works, is dead, being alone" (James 2:17).

7. Guard our conversation. "Let the words of my mouth, and the meditation of my heart, be acceptable in thy sight, O Lord, my strength, and my redeemer" (Psalm 19:14).

8. Focus your eyes on Christ and not on people. "Looking unto Jesus the author and finisher of our faith" (Hebrews 12:2).

9. Walk humbly and trust God. "Humble yourselves therefore under the mighty hand of God, that he may ex-

alt you in due time: Casting all your care upon him; for he careth for you" (I Peter 5:6-7).

10. Grow in grace. "But grow in grace, and in the knowledge of our Lord and Savior Jesus Christ" (II Peter 3:18; also in II Peter 1:1-11. The apostle informs us how to live for God without falling. He concludes by saying, "for if ye do these things, ye shall never fall: For so an entrance shall be ministered unto you abundantly into the everlasting kingdom of our Lord and Savior Jesus Christ."

11. Don't let little debts compound and become a big debt. At our best we need the blood of Jesus Christ to keep us clean. God's Word distinguishes between willful sin and mistakes. God has provided a salvation that will keep us from willful presumptuous sin. Even so, our Lord made a way for one to be reinstated if he or she should fall from the grace of God. Listen to the inspired Word of God: "My little children, these things write I unto you, that ye sin not. And if any man sin, we have an advocate with the Father, Jesus Christ the righteous: And he is the propitiation for our sins: and not for ours only, but also for the sins of the whole world" (I John 2:1-2).

Peter writes that the Lord "is longsuffering to us-ward, not willing that any should perish, but that all should come to repentance" (II Peter 3:9). I have written this book in order to encourage never dying souls, that none will despair, but all may come to our Savior and have eternal life. We as God's people come from various backgrounds and will not always agree on all the details of what I have written but I have prayed for the Holy Spirit to guide me. I am now 92 years old. I have read the Bible through over 60 times, and have stayed close to the Scriptures as I write. If one soul receives help and encouragement from this writing it will be worth the effort.

I find the best way to close this book is quoting from God's Word as recorded in Jude 24-25. "Now unto him that is able to keep you from falling, and to present you faultless before the presence of his glory with exceeding joy, to the only wise God our Savior, be glory and majesty, dominion and power, both now and ever. Amen."